TROPHIES

Challenge Copying Masters

Grade 3 • Volumes 1 and 2

Harcourt
Orlando Boston Dallas Chicago San Diego

Visit *The Learning Site!*
www.harcourtschool.com

rinted in the United States of America

BN 0-15-323521-7

3 4 5 6 7 8 9 10 170 10 09 08 07 06 05 04 03 02

Contents

CHANGING PATTERNS

Contents

ON YOUR MARK

TROPHIES

Volume One

Changing Patterns

Name ______________________________

Word Wise

Even words with similar meanings can convey different messages. Write some sentences, and then see how their messages can change.

department	**obeys**	**commands**	**audience**
expression	**accident**	**noticed**	

What you need:

- pen or pencil
- paper
- index cards

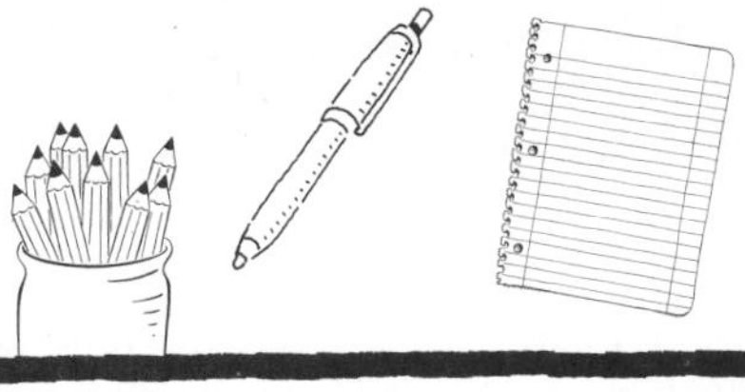

What to do:

1. Write one Vocabulary Word on the front of each card. Brainstorm as many synonyms, or words with similar meanings, as you can for each Vocabulary Word, and write them below the word.

2. Turn each index card over. First, write a sentence using the Vocabulary Word. Next, write the same sentence substituting another word or words for the Vocabulary Word. See how you change the message of the sentence.

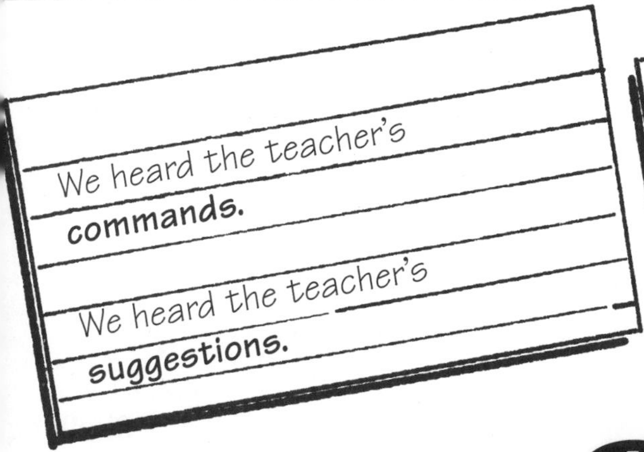
We heard the teacher's
commands.
We heard the teacher's
suggestions.

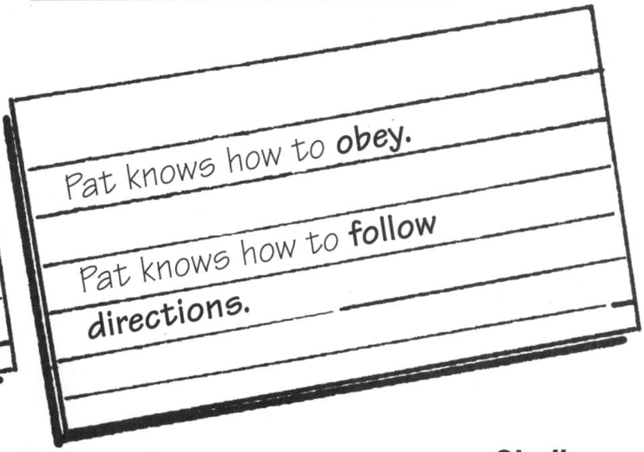
Pat knows how to obey.
Pat knows how to follow
directions.

Name ______________________________

Divide and Conquer!

One way to read a long word is to break it into syllables.

What you need:

- strips of paper 4 inches long by 1 inch wide
- pen or pencil
- scissors
- tape

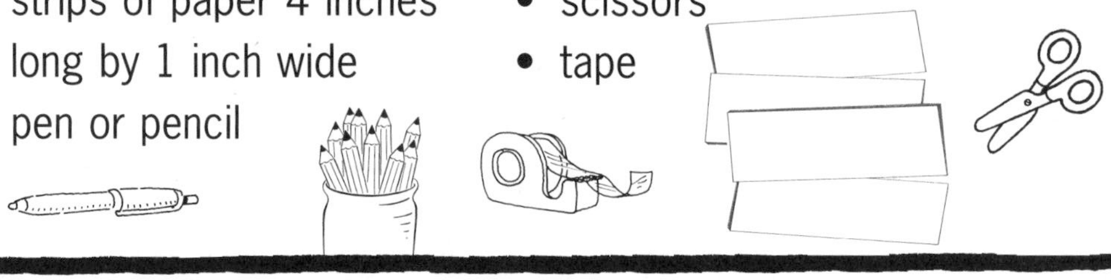

What to do:

1. Write each of the words below on a strip of paper. Then cut apart each word at the lines shown.

de/part/ment
o/beys
com/mands
aud/i/ence
ex/pres/sion
ac/ci/dent
no/ticed

2. Put your word pieces face down, and mix them up. Then put the words back together by joining the correct pieces. Tape your pieces together to show the words you form.

3. Look at the words below. Say each word to yourself slowly. Do you hear each syllable? Divide each word into syllables by drawing lines. Check your answers in a dictionary.

information
auditorium
cellophane
synonym
station
playmate
muscle

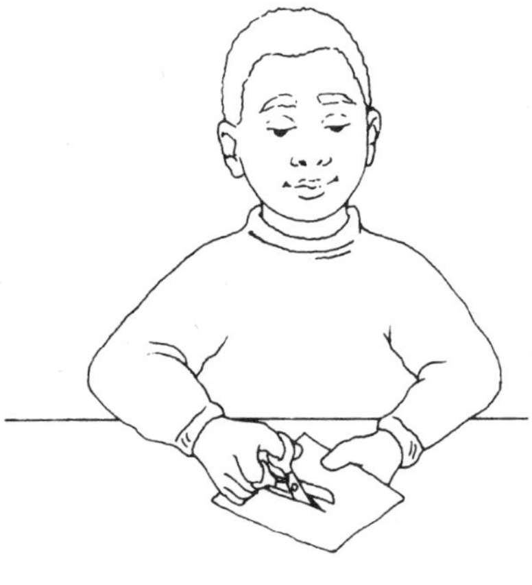

Name ____________________

I Heard That Before!

Pay attention and see how often you come across Vocabulary Words.

grumble exploded languages mumbled streak stubborn darted

What you need:

- pen
- lined paper

What to do:

1. Fold a sheet of paper to make 4 columns. Write the following headings at the top of the columns:
Vocabulary Word
Use It
Hear It
See It
Write the Vocabulary Words in a list in the first column.

2. Keep your paper with you for a whole week. Each time you use a particular Vocabulary Word, put a check mark next to it in the *Use It* column. Write a check mark each time you hear a Vocabulary Word or see it in print.

3. At the end of the week, add up your results. Which word did you *use* most often? Which word did you *hear* most often? Which word did you *see* most often?

Name ______________________________

What a Story!

Every story has *characters*, a *setting*, and a *plot*. Can you create a mixed-up story from familiar stories?

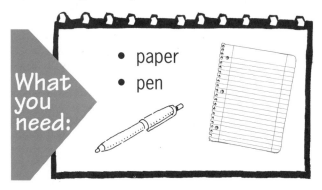

What you need:

- paper
- pen

What to do:

1. Draw a three-column chart on a piece of paper. Write *Characters*, *Setting*, and *Plot* at the top. For each part, write details from a story you've read.

2. Now add the information below to your chart. Think of other familiar stories, and include your own ideas.

Characters	Setting	Plot
Cinderella	palace	loses slipper
Red Riding Hood	forest	visits grandmother
Superman	big city	rescues someone

3. Plan a story by mixing together items from each column. For example:
Superman goes to a palace and loses his slipper.
or
Cinderella goes into the forest and rescues someone.
Then write your story.

Name ______________________________

Dictionary Fun Facts

There's more information in a dictionary than just word meanings. See for yourself.

What you need:

- a dictionary
- paper
- pen

What to do:

1. Number your paper from 1 to 10. Answer the following questions by looking in the dictionary.
   - What does **SOS** stand for?
   - What does the prefix **re-** mean?
   - What does a **gecko** look like?
   - Do **minutemen** work in clock factories?
   - How many syllables does **intelligent** have?
   - Is **kilt** the past tense of kill?
   - How did the **platypus** get its name?
   - Was **Zeus** a real king?
   - What part of speech is **hoax**?
   - Would you find the **Cape of Good Hope** in a closet?

2. Find three other fun facts in the dictionary.

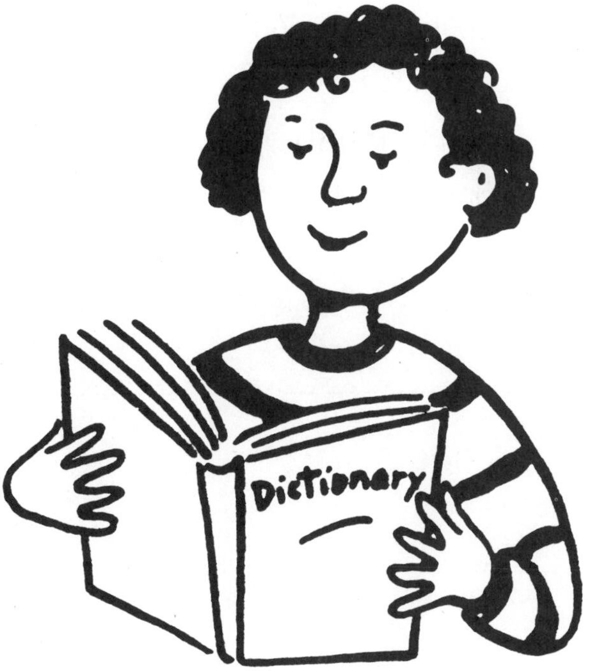

Name ______________________________

What's the Word?

Review the Vocabulary Words by putting them into categories.

case	**specific**	**assistant**	**definitely**
detective	**returned**	**positive**	

What you need:

- paper
- pen

What to do:

1. Copy the following categories on a piece of paper. Write the Vocabulary Word(s) that belong in each category.

People Words
Words That Describe
Feeling Words
Thing Words
Action Words

2. Look through "Nate the Great, San Francisco Detective" to try to find more words. Add words to your paper until you have five examples in each category.

3. Use as many of your Vocabulary Words from your list as you can in a story about a detective. Try to use them based on the way you categorized them.

Name ____________________

Cut Ups!

When you come to long words, look for familiar word parts or spelling patterns.

What you need:

- one-inch strips of paper
- pens or pencil
- scissors
- tape

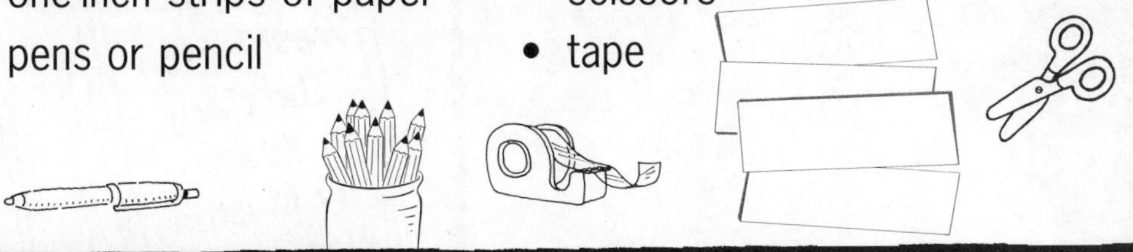

What to do:

1. First, write each word on a strip of paper. Then cut apart each word at the lines shown.

re/turn
bub/ble
re/mark/able
de/tail
un/safe/ly
friend/li/ness

2. Put the pieces face down and mix them up. Then turn over the papers, and form the original words. Tape together the pieces that form the words.

Name ______________________________

Library Scavenger Hunt

Some books give facts and some are pure fiction. Find examples of different kinds of books.

What you need:

- paper and pen
- library

What to do:

1. Look at each kind of book category to the right and its make-believe example. Then think of a real book that fits the category. Write the book's title and author on a piece of paper.

2. Draw twelve squares that will become book covers. Write one real book title and author and one made-up book title and author for each category.

Biography

George Washington: The Early Years by Martha Washington

Nonfiction

Fiction

Mystery

Autobiography

The Story of My Life by I.M. Mee

Poetry

Name ____________________

Word Use

Sort Vocabulary Words from "Allie's Basketball Dream" according to parts of speech.

aimed captain monitor pretended professional familiar

What you need:

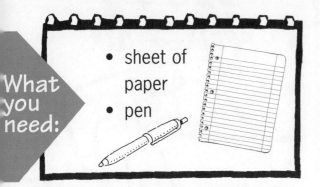

- sheet of paper
- pen

What to do:

1. Fold a sheet of paper into three columns and write the following headings at the top:
   NOUN
   Person, Place, or Thing
   VERB
   Action Word
   ADJECTIVE
   Word That Describes

2. Think about how each Vocabulary Word would be used in a sentence. What part of speech is it? Write words that are nouns in Column One. Write words that are verbs in Column Two. Write words that are adjectives in Column Three.

3. Which Vocabulary Word(s) can be used as two different parts of speech? Write a sentence for each part of speech.

Name ______________________________

Some Character!

Just as you can with people, you can tell what characters are really like by the things they say and do.

What you need:

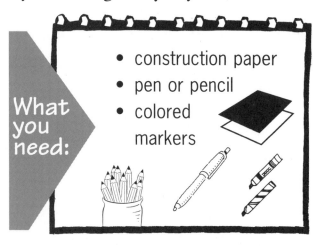

- construction paper
- pen or pencil
- colored markers

What to do:

1. Fold the short side of a sheet of paper in half two times to make four columns. Write the following headings at the top of the columns: *Character*, *Says*, *Does*, and *Conclusion*.

2. Think of the characters from the story you just read. Choose three characters, and write their names in Column One.

3. Look in the story for examples of what each character says and does. Write details in the second and third columns.

4. Now think about each character. What do you conclude? In the last column, tell what you think each character is like.

Name ____________________

Similar or Different?

For every Vocabulary Word, think of words that have similar or different meanings.

ceremonies	**ancient**	**compete**	**host**
earned	**stadium**	**medals**	**record**

What you need:

- paper
- pen or pencil

What to do:

1. Divide your sheet of paper into three equal columns. Write the following headings at the top:
Vocabulary Word
Synonym
Antonym

2. In Column One, list the Vocabulary Words. Next to each word, write either a synonym or an antonym for the word.

3. Make up sentences using each Vocabulary Word. Then make up a sentence for each word's synonym or antonym.

Vocabulary Word	Synonym	Antonym

Name ____________________

It's a Fact

Nonfiction often answers the following questions: *who, what, where, when,* and *how*. Map how well "The Olympic Games" answers these questions.

What you need:

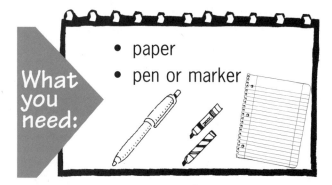

- paper
- pen or marker

What to do:

1. Make a web with a circle in the center and five circles around it.

2. Write the title of the selection in the center of the web. Write a different question word in each of the five circles.

3. Look back at the selection. For each question category, write one question the selection answers. For example: *Who* is Michael Johnson? *When* did the first Olympic Games take place? Then write the answer below each question.

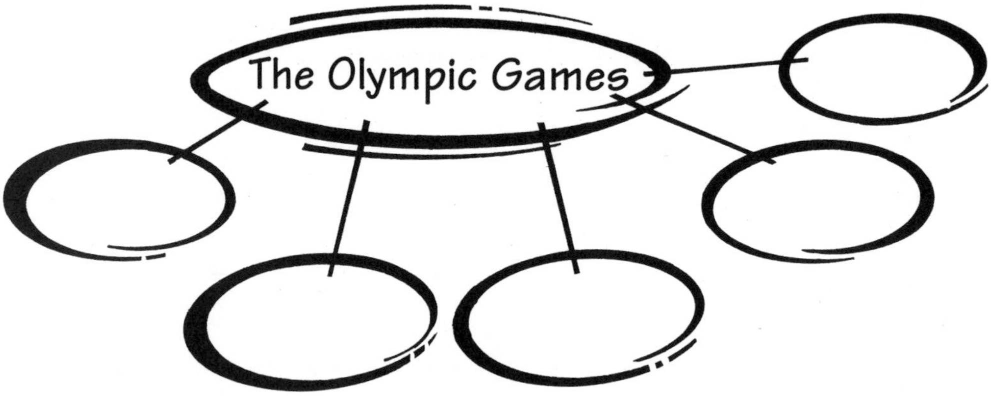

Name ____

What Do You Think?

When you make inferences, you add what you know to what an author tells you. This helps you get more information from your reading.

What you need:

- paper
- markers

What to do:

1. Make a chart with two columns. Label one *What Author Says.* Label the other *What I Know.*

2. In the first column, list something the author says. For example:
At the 2000 Olympic games, 46% of the athletes were women.

3. In the second column, tell something you know that offers more information, for example:

- *There are more women athletes competing today than there were in the past.*
- *More women have become involved in sports in recent years than ever before.*
- *More women's events have been added to the Olympic over the years.*

4. Find two more examples of things the author says. Then add what you know. How does your own knowledge help explain what the author says?

Name ______________________________

Vocabulary Mural

The words and pictures in a book work together to tell a story. You can use pictures to help tell the meanings of words, and create a story at the same time.

trained **wise** **message** **patiently** **litter**

What you need:

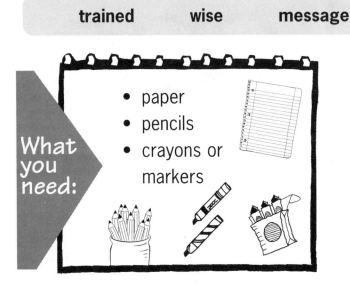

- paper
- pencils
- crayons or markers

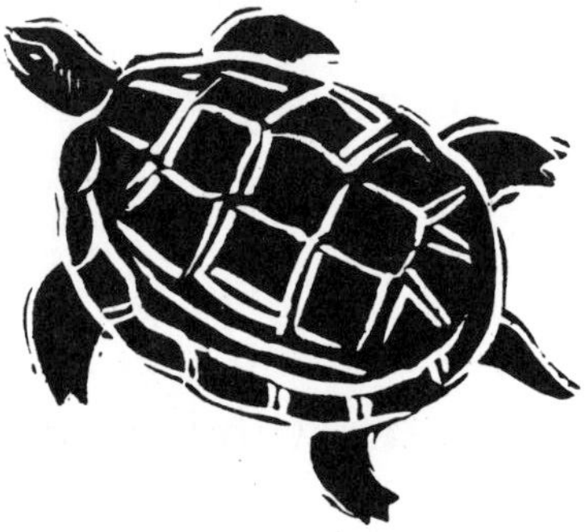

What to do:

1. Use each of the Vocabulary Words in a sentence. The sentences should work together to tell a story or describe a scene. It can be something you made up or something based on "Turtle Bay." You can use more than one Vocabulary Word in the same sentence. You can even try to use all the words in one or two sentences!

2. Draw one picture that tells your story or describes your picture. Include a character or an activity that shows the meaning of each Vocabulary Word. You can show the meaning of a word in different ways—the meaning may be on the expression of a character's face or in the choice of colors.

Name ______________________________

A Different Purpose

The author's purpose for writing is shown by the style of writing, not just the story. You can change a story's purpose just by changing the way you write it.

What you need:

- paper
- pencils
- crayons or markers

What to do:

1. Think of a story you like and know well. It could be a book you just read, a story you read in class, or a fairy tale or folktale. Write down the important events and characters in that story. Then write a short summary of the story.

2. Look at your summary. Decide the purpose of the story. Now retell the story with another purpose. If the story's purpose is to entertain, then tell it as if the purpose were to inform or persuade or explain something.

3. Put a new title on your writing. Make sure the title tells something about the different purpose of your retelling.

Name ____________________

Beach Chart

The beach and the ocean are like a whole other world compared to the city or the country. There are different kinds of plants, animals, sights, and sounds at the beach and in the ocean. You can sort the things you find at the beach in different ways.

What you need:

- paper
- crayons or markers
- travel magazines or newspaper sections
- scissors

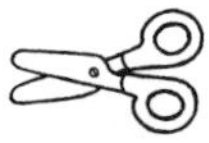

What to do:

1. Begin by brainstorming a list of things you would find at the beach. You may look at "Turtle Bay" or through magazines and newspapers for ideas. Think of sights, sounds, smells, and other things that remind you of the beach.

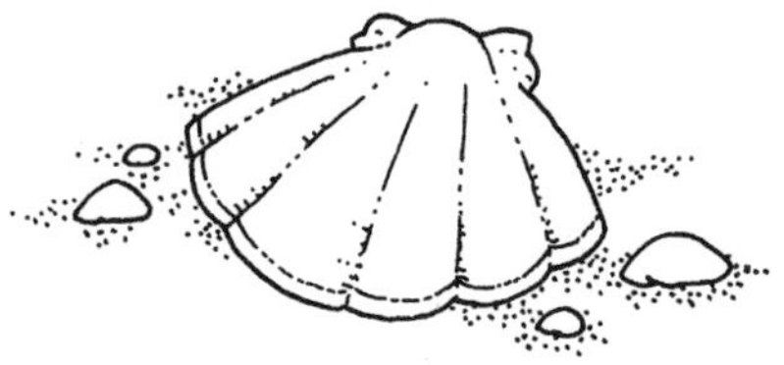

2. Look at your list. What things on your list are alike? How do they belong together? Create categories that go with the items on your list. You can group them in many different ways. You can do *Plants*, *Fish*, *Birds*, and *People*, or you can separate the items by color or size. Make sure that all the items in each category have the same thing in common.

3. Use your list to make a chart. Make one column for each group. At the top of the column, write a title that tells about all the items that belong in that group. Make each category stand out by giving it its own special look. You may choose a different color for each one or use different styles of writing.

Name ____

Dogs with Good Vocabulary

In "Balto, the Dog Who Saved Nome," we hear about the dogs who pull the sled with the medicine, but everything that we hear is from the author. How would the dogs tell it?

telegraph drifts temperature guided trail splinters

What you need:

- paper
- pencils
- crayons or markers

What to do:

1. Think about how and when the Vocabulary Words are used in the story. What is going on? What are the dogs doing?

2. Take your ideas about the dogs, and turn them into a comic strip that tells the story from the point of view of the dogs. Tell about what happens in each frame, using voice balloons, captions, and pictures. Use each of the Vocabulary Words at least once.

Name ____________________________________

Slogans and Symbols

There are many tricky kinds of words. Some may be spelled alike but sound different and have different meaning. Others may sound the same but have different spellings. Some have multiple meanings. Others mean the same or opposite of words you know. How can you keep all the types straight? Advertisers know that catchy symbols and phrases help people remember things.

What you need:

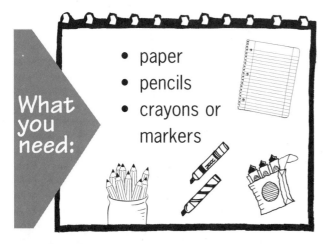

- paper
- pencils
- crayons or markers

What to do:

1. Look at different categories of words: *homophones*, *homographs*, *multiple-meaning words*, *synonyms* and *antonyms*. Make sure you understand what they mean. Write each of these categories on a sheet of paper. Leave plenty of space next to each one.

2. Imagine that you were making up an ad for each type of word. What kind of catchy slogan would go with that type? It should tell what that type of word is like but be short and easy to remember. For example: "Means the Same, Different Name!" for synonyms. Write your slogan next to each word type. Include a few examples for a reminder.

3. Advertisements also have pictures or designs that help you remember. Think of a picture or design for each word type. Draw it next to your slogan.

Name ______________________________

Finding Clues

Pictures, titles, and chapter headings can help you predict the next part of a story. In fact, sometimes you can learn a lot just by looking at the cover of a book!

What you need:

- books or magazines
- paper
- pencil
- crayons or markers

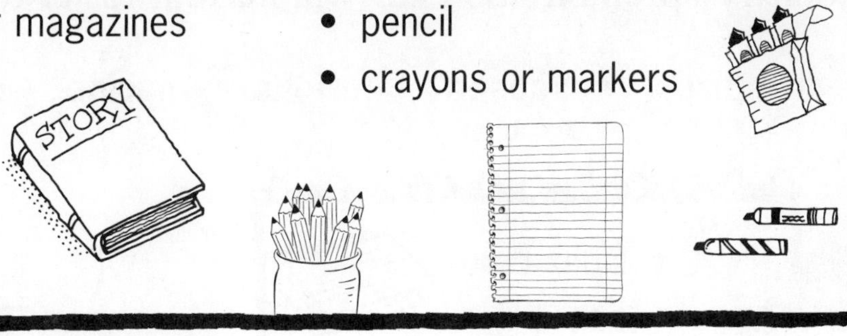

What to do:

1. Find some books or magazine articles you have not read.

2. Look carefully at the titles and pictures. What do you see? Are the words mysterious or clear? Is the title the name of a person or place? Are there characters in the pictures? What are they doing? Write a few sentences that tell what you think the book or article is about.

3. Check your predictions by reading the book flap or a few paragraphs of the article. What did you get right? What did you get wrong? Now that you know something about the story, can you see clues that could have helped you make the right prediction?

Name ______________________________

Pronunciation Power

The best way to find out a word's pronunciation is to look in a dictionary. Next to each word are symbols and letters that show how to pronounce the word. At the bottom of most dictionary pages, there is a key that tells what sounds these symbols and letters make. Learning how to use a dictionary's pronunciation key will make it easier to sound out new words.

creature collapsed curious marine delicate survived

What you need:

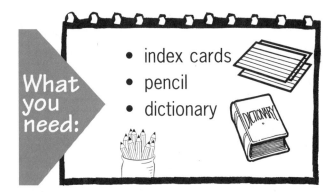

- index cards
- pencil
- dictionary

What to do:

1. Write each Vocabulary Word on an index card.

2. Look up each word in the dictionary. Now look at the pronunciation next to the word. Look at the symbols and letters. Then study the pronunciation key on the dictionary page. Use the key to sound out each part of the word. Write the pronunciation on the card with the word and its meaning.

3. Think of words you know that have similar spellings. Look them up in the dictionary and check their pronunciations. If they have the same pronunciation, write them on the back of that word's card. Start a new pronunciation card if a word is pronounced differently.

4. Keep your cards together and use them as a reference for pronouncing challenging words.

Name ______________________________

Visit the Galapagos Islands!

Tui de Roy uses her writing and pictures to *inform* and to *express* how she feels. Another reason for writing is to *persuade*. When you write to persuade, you give reasons for why someone should do something or agree with you about an issue. What if Tui de Roy had written "Wild Shots, They're My Life" to persuade?

What you need:

- pencils
- paper
- crayons or markers
- travel magazines
- scissors
- glue or tape

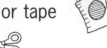

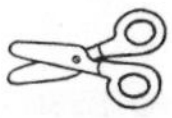

What to do:

1. Look through "Wild Shots, They're My Life." Make a list of things you like about it. You may write down pictures that catch your attention, interesting information, or things that seem fun. What does your list tell you about the Galapagos Islands? Use your list to persuade others to visit there.

2. Create a travel brochure or an ad for a trip to the Galapagos Islands. Write a brief paragraph that gives reasons why someone would want to go there. Tell what they would see and do while visiting. Look through travel magazines to see how their ads catch people's interest.

3. Decorate your brochure or ad. You can draw your own pictures, or copy the ones from the selection. You can also cut pictures out of magazines and glue or tape them to your paper.

Name ______________________________

Word Problems

A word's definition is a group of words that "add up" to that one word. You can make a "math sentence" out of any word.

brunch **omelet** **peaceful** **erupting** **lava** **escape**

What you need:
- pencil
- paper

What to do:

1. Think of words related to each of the Vocabulary Words. They can be words with the same meaning, words that describe it, or words that are often used with the Vocabulary Word. Write down as many as you can.

2. Now choose two or three words for each Vocabulary Word. Draw a picture for each word, with plus signs in between. They should "equal" the Vocabulary Word.

3. Show your word problems to a friend. Cover the answer, and see if your friend can figure out which Vocabulary Word is the sum of your word pictures.

Name ______________________________

Word Pairs

Homophones have different spellings and meanings but are related because they sound the same. Homographs are related because they are spelled the same, although they have different meanings and pronunciations.

What you need:

- index cards
- pencil
- crayons or markers

What to do:

1. Think of three pairs of homophones. Use one index card for each pair. Write one word and its definition on the front. Write the other word and its definition on the back. Do the same for the other pairs.

2. Think of three pairs of homographs. Write one word, its definition, and its phonetic respelling on the front. Write the same information for the other word on the back. Do the same for the other pairs.

Name ______________________________

Vocabulary Haikus

A haiku is a three-line poem that does not rhyme. All the words in the first line add up to five syllables. The words in the second line add up to seven syllables. The last line also totals five syllables. A haiku can be about anything you like. It may be made of words that remind you of something or words that tell how you feel.

approach	**confident**	**comfortable**	**firm**
program	**equipment**	**appointment**	

What you need:

- paper
- pencil
- crayons or markers

What to do:

1. Use each Vocabulary Word in its own haiku. First count the number of syllables in each word. Write that down next to each word, so you know how many syllables that word will use up.

2. Write your haikus. Remember, the first line is five syllables, the second is seven syllables, and the third is five syllables. Each haiku should tell something about what the Vocabulary Word means or what that word makes you think about. You can even use the word the way it is used in Rosie's story.

3. Draw a picture to go with each haiku.

Name ______________________________

Word Flash

Long words are usually built from pieces. Sometimes, the beginning piece is a *prefix*, the middle piece is a *root*, and the end piece is a *suffix*. When you know the meanings of these pieces, you can figure out the meanings of many big words.

What you need:

- index cards
- paper
- pencil

- clock or watch
- dictionary

What to do:

1. Write each of the prefixes and suffixes listed below on an index card.

Prefixes	Suffixes
un-	-ion
re-	-tion
in-	-ation
im-	-ible
ir-	-able
il-	-ness
dis-	-ity
en-	-ment
em-	-ous
non-	-eous
over-	-ive
mis-	-ful
sub-	-less
pre-	-est

2. Place the stack of index cards face down. When you turn over a card, write down as many words using that prefix or suffix as you can. Using what you know about prefixes and suffixes, write down a definition of each word. Use a dictionary if you need help. How many words can you write and define in fifteen minutes?

Name ______________________________

One Thing Leads to Another

In a story, one event leads to the next. Can you create a story out of a group of unconnected words?

cartwheel seriously mustache fastened beyond collection

What you need:

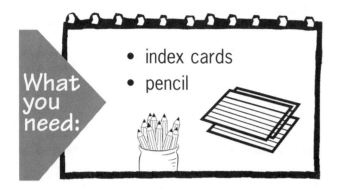

- index cards
- pencil

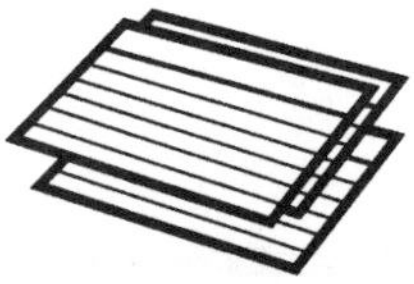

What to do:

1. Write a sentence for each Vocabulary Word on separate index cards. The sentence should show the meaning of the Vocabulary Word.

2. Look at your six sentences. Arrange the cards in different orders until they make sense as a story.

3. Rewrite the sentences as a story, using the order in which you placed the cards. You may add time-order words such as *first*, *next*, *then*, *after*, *later*, and *finally*.

Name ____

Pieces of Story

Stories need to be in an order that makes sense. Can you put the pieces of a story in the right order?

What you need:

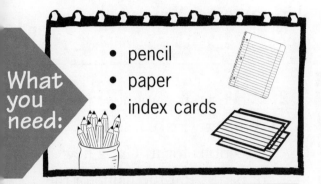

- pencil
- paper
- index cards

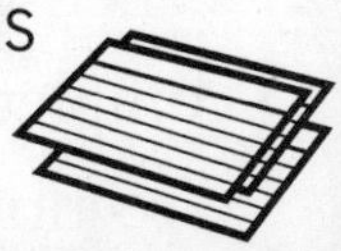

What to do:

1. Think of a story that you know well, or make one up. Write down the important events on a sheet of paper. If you have trouble remembering something, ask yourself, "And then what happened?"

2. Look at your list of events. Is that everything? Are they in an order that makes sense? Now write each event on its own index card. Use words such as *first*, *next*, *then*, *now*, and *finally* to help tell when in the story each event takes place.

3. Shuffle your cards, and trade with a partner. Each of you can try to put the other's story in order. When you're finished, use the cards to read the story aloud to your partner.

Name ______________________________

Teach Your Own Game

When you want to play a new game, it helps to follow directions. Directions need to be in the right order, or they are not very useful. They should tell every step and not skip anything. You can also use directions to teach someone a new game.

What you need:

- paper
- pencil
- crayons or markers

What to do:

1. Think of a completely new game, or base a new game on one that you already know. Think about what people need to play the game, how many people can play it, where it is played, and each step needed to play it. Jot all your ideas down on paper.

2. When your game idea is complete, make a set of directions for it. Use a new sheet of paper. Put the name of the game at the top. Think of a fun sounding name that will make people want to play it. Then write down what players need, how many players there should be, and where to play it.

3. List the directions in step-by-step order. Write each step simply and clearly. Use words such as *first*, *next*, *then*, and *finally* to keep the steps in order. You can also number each step.

4. Use markers or crayons to draw pictures next to each step. The pictures should show each step.

Name ____________________

Come to the Show!

If you were putting on a school talent show, you would have to let people know when it was happening, where it was happening, and why they should come to it. Tell about a talent show!

gym perform prefer recite enjoying billions roam

What you need:

- poster paper
- crayons or markers

What to do:

1. Look at your Vocabulary Words. Make sure you know what each word means and that you are comfortable using each word in a sentence.

2. Use your Vocabulary Words in a poster that will advertise a school talent show. You may use them to tell where it will take place or to describe some of the acts in the show. You can use lots of other words, too, but you should use at least five of your Vocabulary Words. Remember, you are describing your own talent show, not the one in the story.

Name ______________________________

Prefix/Suffix Land

When you know the meanings of prefixes and suffixes, you can figure out almost any word. Picture a place where you can see all prefixes and suffixes and learn what they mean.

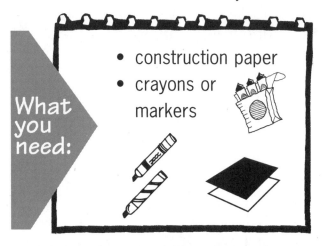

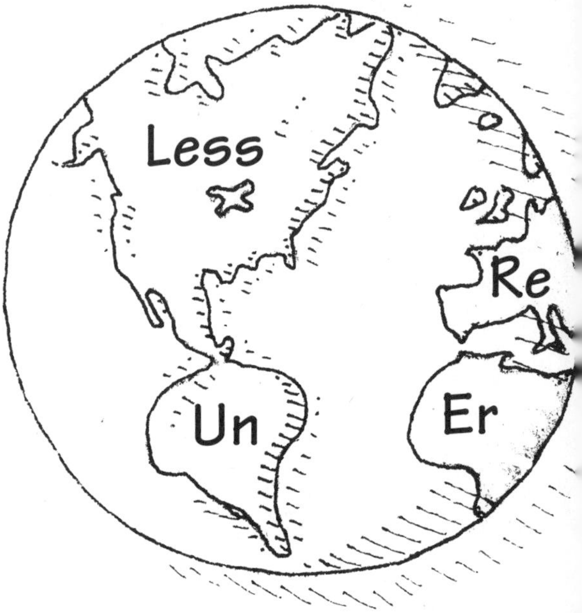

What you need:

- construction paper
- crayons or markers

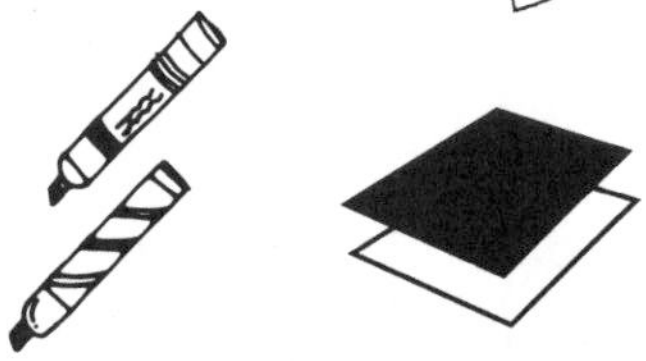

What to do:

1. Make a list of prefixes and suffixes, for example *un-*, *re-*, *in-*, *-ness*, *-er*, *-ment*, and *-tion*. Find out what each of them means.

2. Take a piece of construction paper. Think of it as a map of a world. Draw countries of all shapes and sizes on the paper.

3. Name each country after a prefix or suffix. Write the prefix or suffix and its meaning on its country. Write words that use that prefix or suffix throughout its country. Those are the cities.

4. Keep your prefix/suffix map, and use it when you need to figure out the meaning of a word!

Name ______________________________

Solve a Mystery

A story or a picture may not tell you everything, but it may give you clues that let you find your own answers. When you ask yourself questions, you can find clues and then solve the mystery.

What you need:

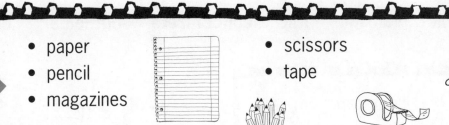

- paper
- pencil
- magazines
- scissors
- tape

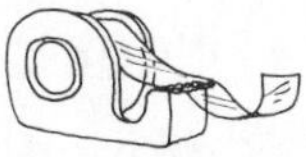

What to do:

1. Look through some magazines. Find a picture that seems interesting. It can be a picture from an ad or from an article.

2. Cut out the picture. Tape it to a piece of paper. Underneath the picture, write the word *Clues*.

3. Next to the word *Clues*, write down all the pieces of information you get from looking at the picture. If it's a picture of people, you may notice where they are, what they are doing, how old they are, and what kind of clothes they are wearing. If it's a picture of a thing, you may notice where it is, what size and color it is, and what other things are around it.

4. Look at your list of clues. What do they tell you, and how do they all add up? Write a brief paragraph that tells your conclusion about the picture.

Name ______________________________

Start a Baseball Team

The baseball players on Jose's team have nicknames, but we don't find out how they got them. A nickname usually tells something about a person—how they look, or what they do. Any word can be a nickname.

ballhawk   vanish   fault   concentrate   outfielder   depend

What you need:

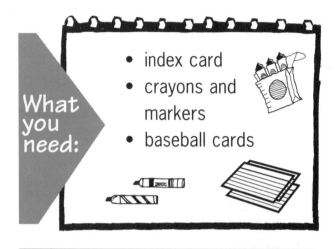

- index card
- crayons and markers
- baseball cards

What to do:

1. Write nicknames for baseball players using the Vocabulary Words, for example: "Concentrate Jones."

2. Now write sentences telling the reason why a player would have that nickname. The reason should show the meaning of the word.

3. Create a baseball card for each of your players. You can draw a picture of the player at bat, or throwing or catching a ball. Look at a real baseball card if you need ideas. Under the picture, write the name of the player and the player's position. Below that, write the reason for the player's nickname.

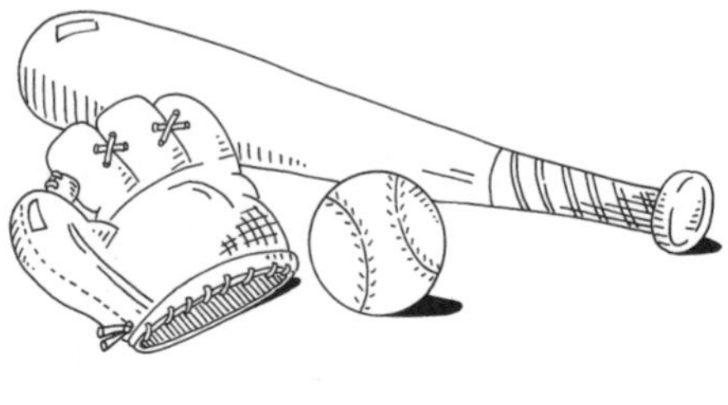

Name ____

Write a Sports Report

The beginning of "Centerfield Ballhawk" tells about the baseball game between Jose's team, the Mudders, and the Bulls. We see the baseball game from Jose's point of view. How would a sports reporter tell about the game?

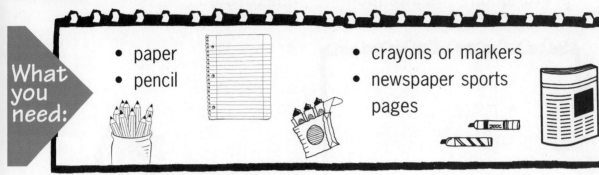

What you need:

- paper
- pencil

- crayons or markers
- newspaper sports pages

What to do:

1. Reread the description of the baseball game in "Centerfield Ballhawk." Write down each important event as you read it. Include who comes up to bat, what kind of hit the batter makes, and what the score is at the time.

2. Now use the details to write an article about the game. Use time-order words such as *first*, *then*, *next*, and *finally* to keep the events in order. Use descriptive words to make your article exciting. Look at the sports pages in a newspaper for ideas.

3. Use markers to create a big, bold headline for your story. Think of an exciting title that will catch readers' attention.

Name ______________________________

Call the Doctor!

Some of the most exciting TV shows and movies are about doctors and hospitals. What if you had a chance to write one of these shows?

glanced **comfort** **longed** **contagious**
prescription **attention** **unexpected**

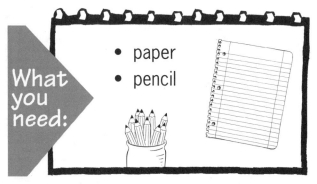

What you need:

- paper
- pencil

What to do:

1. Write a scene that takes place in a hospital or a doctor's office. It can be between two doctors, a doctor and a nurse, a doctor and a patient, or any two characters you want. Use each Vocabulary Word at least once.

2. Use dialogue and stage directions to tell what happens in the scene. Remember, a scene should have a beginning, a middle, and an ending.

3. Share your scene with a partner. Work together to act out your scene!

Name ______________________________

School of Prefixes and Suffixes

Groups of fish that travel together are called schools of fish. With your help, groups of words that have the same prefixes or suffixes can travel in schools, too!

What you need:

- paper
- pencil

- poster paper
- crayons or markers

What to do:

1. Choose two prefixes such as *re-*, *un-*, *dis-*, and *pre-*. Then choose two suffixes such as *-tion*, *-er*, *-ness*, *-less*, and *-ful*. Write your two prefixes and two suffixes on a piece of paper. Find out what your prefixes or suffixes mean when added to a word.

2. Brainstorm a list of words that use those prefixes and suffixes. Write down as many as you can. If you need ideas, look in a dictionary. Make sure you know what each word means.

3. Now design a fish for each group of words. Think of a fish shape and color. Sketch out your designs on regular paper.

4. On poster paper, draw a school of each type of fish. In each fish, write one of the words from your list.

5. Add plants, shells, and other underwater life to decorate your poster.

Name ________________________________

Translate Proverbs

As you saw in your reading, the same proverb can be said in many different ways. It still has the same meaning, though. You can create your own way of saying a proverb.

generations	**persistently**	**illuminated**
summons	**faithful**	**fortunate**

What you need:

- paper
- pencils
- crayons or markers
- hole punch
- string or yarn
- book of proverbs

What to do:

1. Look at your Vocabulary Words. Use them to rewrite proverbs. Look through "Sayings We Share" or a book of proverbs for ideas. If you see a word in a proverb that is a synonym for one of the Vocabulary Words, you should choose to rewrite that proverb.

2. Once you have chosen a proverb, think of a way to say the same thing using the Vocabulary Word. For example, *If at first you don't succeed, try, try again* might become *If at first you fail, work* ***persistently*** *until you succeed.*

3. Write each revised proverb on a separate sheet of paper. Draw a picture to go with it. The picture should help show what the proverb means. Collect your sheets of proverbs in a stack and punch a hole in one corner. Tie a piece of string or yarn through the hole to make a booklet.

Name ______________________________

Your Favorite Story Parts

Every story has a plot that tells what happens, characters that act out the plot, and a setting where it takes place. Which elements do you like best about your favorite stories?

What you need:

- paper
- pencil
- crayons or markers

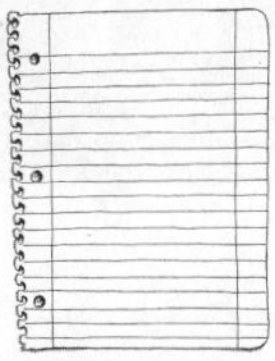

What to do:

1. Think of your favorite books or stories. Choose two of them.

2. Make a three-column chart. Choose three different colored markers or crayons. Use one color to label a column *Plot*, another color to label a column *Characters*, and a third color to label a column *Setting*.

3. Divide your chart into two rows. Put the name of one story next to the first row, and the name of the other story next to the second row.

4. Fill in the columns, using information from each of your stories. Make sure you use the same colors throughout each column. For the *Plot* column, write about the most important events in the plot. For the *Characters* column, describe the most important characters. For the *Setting* column, list where and when the story takes place.

	Plot	Characters	Setting
Story 1			
Story 2			

TROPHIES

Volume Two

On Your Mark

Name ______________________________

Vocabulary Wanted

Where would you look if you wanted to find a job, or buy a used car, or find out where there are garage sales? You would look in the *classified* section of the newspaper. An ad in the classified section tells what a person wants to sell or wants to buy or tells what job a person wants or what job is available.

colonel soldiers brambles weary outstretched stumbling urgent

What you need:

- paper
- pencil
- scissors
- tape
- newspapers—classified section

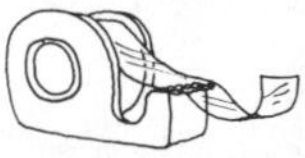

What to do:

1. Make sure you understand what each Vocabulary Word means.

2. Write at least three classified ads, using more than one Vocabulary Word in each ad if possible. Look at the classified section of a newspaper if you need ideas.

3. Draw columns on a piece of paper. Put a heading across the top that reads *Classified Pages.* Make a heading for each column that tells what type of ad is found there. It could be *Help Wanted* or *For Sale*. If all your ads are in the same category, you will only need one heading.

4. Cut out your ads, and tape them under the right headings. If you have more than one ad in a column, make sure they are listed in alphabetical order.

Name ______________________________

Action! Comic Book Summary

A comic book tells a story using pictures and few words. Each panel *sums up* an event or moment in the story. Make your own comic book!

What you need:

- paper
- pencil
- crayons or markers

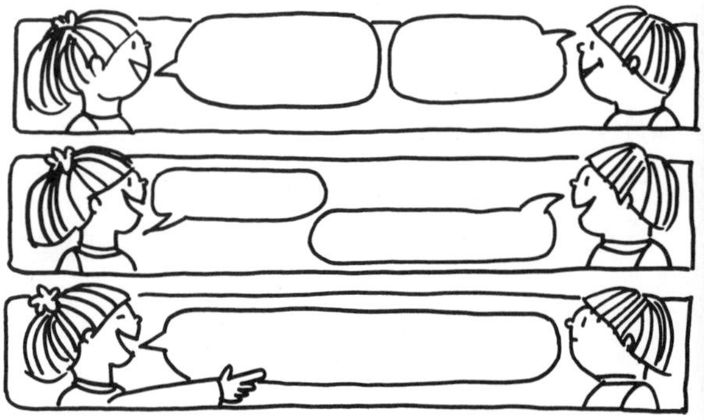

What to do:

1. Reread "Papa Tells Chita a Story". Find the places where Chita interrupts her father with a comment or a question. Using those interruptions, break the story into sections.

2. Write a one-sentence summary for each section. Make sure you sum up all the action that happens in that section. Don't include any details that aren't about the action.

3. Use your summaries to make Papa's story into a comic book. Write each one-sentence summary in a panel of the story. You can add to each panel by having characters speak to each other in voice balloons. Make sure you keep the action in order and that you don't skip any sections.

4. Use crayons or markers to color your comic book. Color will make it more interesting to read.

Name ______________________________

A Dictionary of Sounds

***Onomatopoeia* is the use of words to create a sound. The word *meow* uses spelling and pronunciation to copy the sound a cat makes. *Shhh* is also onomatopoeia. How many onomatopoeia words can you think of?**

What you need:

- paper
- pencil
- crayons or markers

What to do:

1. Think of words whose sounds tell what they mean. If you have trouble getting started, try to think of sounds that animals and insects make. Then think of sounds that go with weather, such as the sounds of thunder or rain. Write down as many words as you can.

2. Now use your list to make a dictionary. Put your onomatopoeia words in alphabetical order. Next to each one, write a definition, such as *The sound a cat makes*. Leave space between each word, so that you have room to add more words.

3. Add drawings to your dictionary. If you used more than one sheet of paper, put them together to make a booklet. Call it your *Onomatopoeia Dictionary*.

Name ______________________________

Vocabulary Stars

In "Coyote Places the Stars," Coyote arranges the stars in the sky in the shape of animals. If you were making a constellation of stars, what shape would you make?

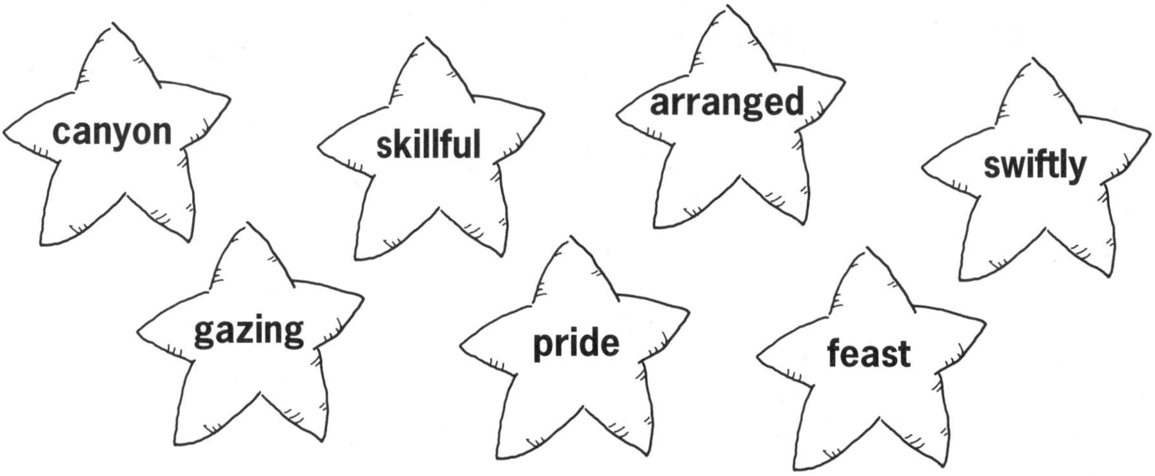

What you need:

- pencil
- paper

What to do:

1. Make a constellation out of each Vocabulary Word. Use one piece of paper for each word. Draw a star for each letter, and write the letter on the star. Arrange the stars in any pattern you like. Try to choose something that reminds you of the meaning of the word.

2. Below your constellation, write a sentence that uses the word.

Name ______________________________

Something in Common

Everyone has things they like and dislike. Chances are that the things you like have something in common with each other.

What you need:

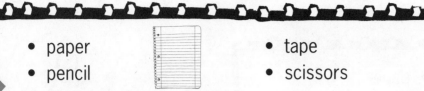

- paper
- pencil
- old magazines
- tape
- scissors

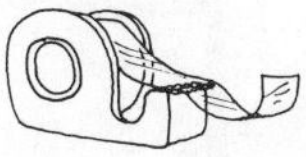
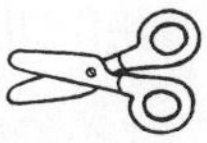

What to do:

1. Look through some magazines. Find two pictures that interest you, and cut them out. Fold a piece of paper into three sections. Tape one picture to the top of the first section. Tape the other picture to the top of the third section. Write *Different* underneath each picture. In the center section, write *Alike*.

2. Look carefully at the pictures. At first they may seem very different. Write what is different about them under each picture. For example, one may be of an animal, while the other might be of a person.

3. Look carefully at your pictures again. If both of these caught your attention, they must have something in common. They may have the same colors, or they may both be pictures of sports. Write what is alike about the pictures in the center section.

4. At the bottom of the page write a summary of what you found. What does this compare and contrast exercise tell about the things you like?

Name ______________________________

Discover a Bug

What if you discovered a bug that no one had ever seen before?

nonsense tidbit mischief duty council satisfied

What you need:

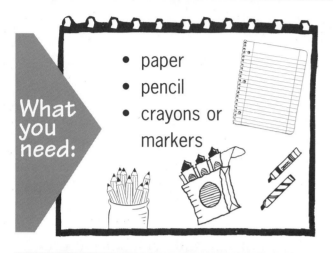

- paper
- pencil
- crayons or markers

What to do:

1. Imagine a bug. It should be like an insect, not like an animal or a person. Try to think of an insect you know, such as an ant or a bee. Then think of how you would change that insect to make it more exciting or interesting. You can also combine several insects to make a super bug.

2. Draw your bug on a piece of paper. Use color to make it interesting.

3. Now imagine that you are writing the encyclopedia entry for the new bug you have discovered. Use your Vocabulary Words to describe what it looks like, what it does, and what is special about it.

Name ______________________________

Make Your Movie

When people make a movie, they begin by creating storyboards to show what will happen in each scene. The storyboards *summarize* the action. See if you can plan your own movie by summarizing the action.

What you need:

- paper
- pencil
- crayons or markers

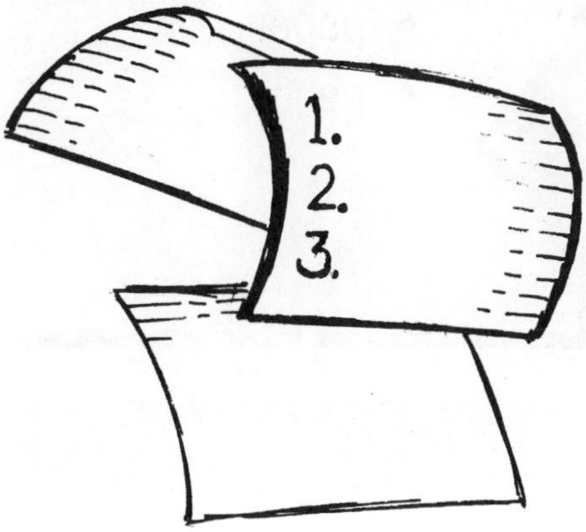

What to do:

1. Think of a story you like and know well. Write down all the important events. Include only the events and action that help to tell the story. You don't need to include descriptions of characters and settings. Number the events to keep them in order.

2. Divide your paper into six boxes. Make sure each box is big enough for you to draw and write in.

3. In the first box, draw a sketch that shows what happens in your first event. Write a very brief sentence that tells what happens. Fill in the rest of the boxes, putting one event in each box. Start a new sheet of paper if you need more than six boxes.

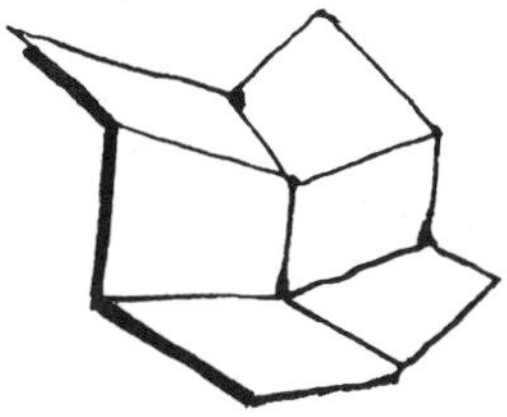

Name ______________________________

Newsbreak

Clever Children Outsmart Wolf

latch dusk cunning embraced tender brittle delighted

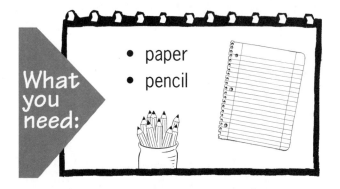

What you need:

- paper
- pencil

What to do:

1. Imagine that you are a reporter who has just found out about the Lon Po Po story. You have interviewed the children and heard about their experience with the wolf.

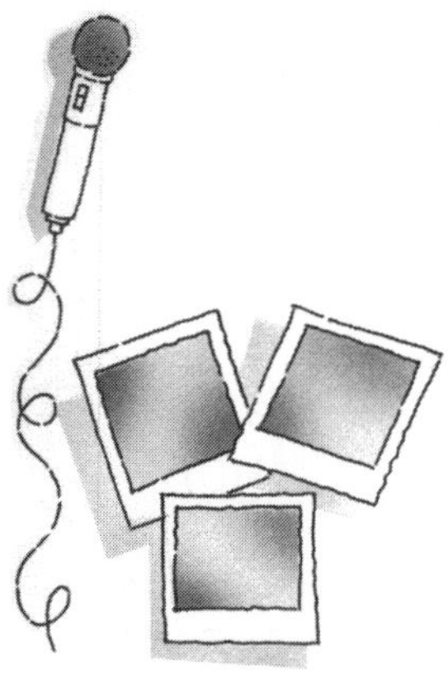

2. Write a report that tells about the story for the evening news. Use all the Vocabulary Words to help tell the story. Think of an opening that will get your audience's attention. Make sure that you sum up the events from beginning to end. Stick to the facts, but keep your story interesting. Include comments from the girls that tell how they felt while the action was happening.

3. Read your story aloud. Speak clearly like a real newscaster.

Name ____

The Meeting

Think about your favorite characters from stories and books you've read. What if they met?

What you need:

- paper
- pencil

What to do:

1. Think of two favorite characters. Make lists of everything you know about them, such as what they look like, what they do, and what they like or dislike.

2. Look at both of your lists. Circle things that are alike. Underline things that are different.

3. Use the information from your lists to write a dialogue between the two characters. Imagine that they are meeting for the first time. Think of a place where the two might meet, such as at a party, in line at the store, or at your house. Have them ask each other questions to find out how they are alike and how they are different.

Name ______________________________

House of Words

If all the Vocabulary Words lived together, would each one get its own room?

wits wailing advice dreadful faring farewell

What you need:

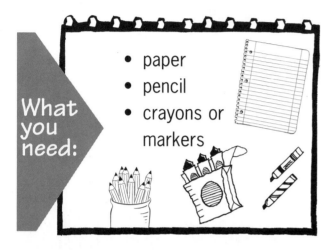

- paper
- pencil
- crayons or markers

What to do:

1. Draw boxes to build a house. Each box should represent a room. The way you lay them out on the page is the layout of the house. For example, the first floor might have four boxes next to each other, and the second floor might be two boxes on top of those.

2. You can use one box for each Vocabulary Word, or you can make some words share rooms. Decide if you want a very open house or a crowded house.

3. Write each Vocabulary Word and a sentence that shows the meaning of the word. If you put more than one word in a room, write sentences telling how the words would get along with each other.

4. Color and decorate your house however you'd like!

Name ____

Scene Again

"The Crowded House" both entertains and teaches a lesson. Just changing the words, however, can change the purpose of the story.

What you need:

- pencil
- paper

What to do:

1. Choose a scene from "The Crowded House." Rewrite the scene three ways: to persuade, to inform, and to give directions. For example, you may have one of the characters try to persuade another to agree to something; you may have a character explain something to another; or you may have characters give step-by-step directions about how to do something.

2. Make sure that your versions of the scene give the same information as the original. You can add new things, but the scene should still fit into the same place in the play. You can change the writing purpose just by changing words and point of view!

Name ______________________________

Go to the Auction!

In "Leah's Pony," there is an auction to raise money by selling the family's belongings. There are real auctions all over the world where people sell fantastic things for millions of dollars, such as paintings and antique furniture. What would it be like at one of these auctions?

glistened   county   galloped   clutched   bid   auctioneer

What you need:

- paper
- pencils
- crayons or markers
- magazines (about antiques or auctions if possible)

What to do:

1. Imagine that you are at an auction. All kinds of things might be for sale—antique furniture, jewelry, paintings, sports items. Make a list of things you might see at the auction. Look through magazines if you need ideas.

2. Using your Vocabulary Words, write sentences that tell about what it is like at the auction. Your sentences can describe what you would see or things you might hear people say at an auction. You might hear and see people who are trying to buy things and people who are trying to sell things.

3. Draw a picture to go with your sentences.

Name ______________________________

Buyer Beware

A fact can be proven or disproven, but an opinion is just what someone believes. Advertisements may contain both facts and opinions. Can you tell which is which?

What you need:

- magazines
- paper
- pencil
- tape
- scissors

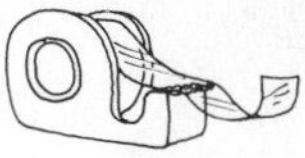

What to do:

1. Look through magazine advertisements. Cut out some that have *facts* in them. Advertisements with facts will show that a product has been tested. There may be numbers that prove the product worked, or pictures that show the results of the product.

2. Cut out advertisements that have *opinions*. Advertisements that have opinions will say things such as "the best ever" or "the most fantastic." These statements cannot be proven or disproven since they are people's opinions.

3. Write how you know which ads have facts and which have opinions. Do any have both?

Name ____

Letters from Out West

What if you spent a summer on a ranch?

ranchers profit tending corral stray market

What you need:

- paper
- pencil
- crayons or markers

What to do:

1. Imagine that you are spending a summer on a ranch. Based on what you read in the story, write down ideas of things you might see and do.

2. Using your list, write a letter to a friend that describes your life on the ranch. Use each of your Vocabulary Words at least once. Try to write sentences that show what they mean.

3. Draw a picture that shows the things you wrote about.

Name ______________________________

Support a Main Idea

Everything you read has a main idea. The details in a piece help support the main idea. What main ideas and supporting details have you seen when you read?

What you need:

- paper
- pencil
- books or magazines you like

What to do:

1. Find a book, story, or magazine article that you like. Choose three or four different paragraphs. Read them carefully.

2. Fold a piece of paper in half. Write the words *Main Idea* at the top of one half and *Supporting Details* at the top of the other.

3. Look at each of your paragraphs. In the *Main Idea* column, write what you think is the main idea of each paragraph. In the *Supporting Details* column, write the details from the paragraph that support or explain the main idea.

4. When you are finished, look at your list of main ideas. What do they tell you about the main idea of the book, story, or article? Write what you think it is at the bottom of the page.

Name ____

Informative Animals

Encyclopedias, dictionaries, and thesauruses can all help you find specific kinds of information. It can take all three, however, to get a complete picture of a subject.

What you need:

- encyclopedia
- dictionary
- thesaurus

- paper
- pencil
- crayons

What to do:

1. Think of an animal that you are interested in. Use one of your three reference sources to find information about that animal. Write down three interesting facts that you find in your research.

2. List any unfamiliar words that you find while doing your research. Use one of your three reference sources to find out the meanings of these words. Then find synonyms for the words you just looked up. You may not find synonyms for each of the unfamiliar words, but write down what you find.

3. On another sheet of paper, draw or trace a large outline of the animal you researched. In the body of the animal, write down the three interesting facts you found. Near the head of the animal, write down the unfamiliar words and their meanings. Underneath each of those words, write the synonyms you found.

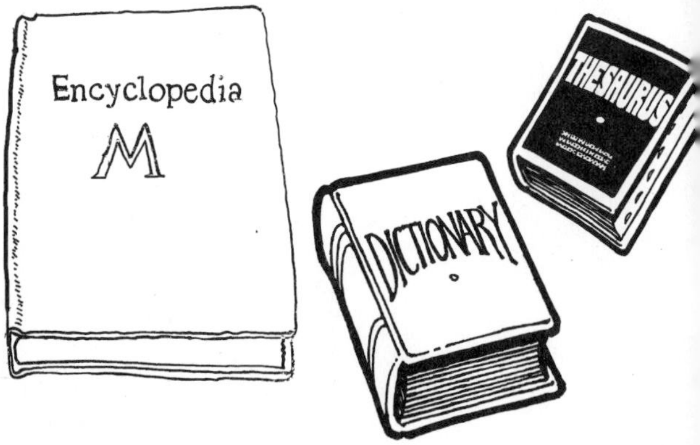

Name ______________________________

A Brand New Town!

f you were just starting a new town, you would need to try to get ›eople to come live there. How would you attract them?

stagecoach	**miners**	**nuggets**	**skillet**
settle	**boom town**	**landmark**	

What you need:

- pencils
- paper
- crayons or markers

What to do:

1. Draw a map of your new town. Make sure you include places where people can get the things they need, just like in the story "Boom Town." Give your town a name.

2. Underneath, write an ad inviting people to come live in your town. Tell why it will be a good place to live. Use each of your Vocabulary Words at least once. You can use them as part of the ad or as names for places on the map of your town.

Name ____

That's My Opinion!

You have your own opinions about things. However, if you use facts to support that opinion, you may be able to get others to agree with you.

What you need:

- paper
- pencil
- reference books
- magazines

What to do:

1. Choose a game you like to play. Write down why it is a great game and what you like about it. Include why you think it's fun and why you think other people would find it fun. Then write down important facts about the game. These can include what you need to play it, how many people can play, and how it is played.

2. Draw a picture of people playing your game. Underneath your picture, write *Opinion* and *Fact*. Under *Opinion*, write down all the reasons you like it and why other people would like it. Under *Fact*, write down all the important things about the game, such as how to play it and what is needed to play it.

3. Look at your facts and opinions. Do the facts of the game help support your opinion that it's a great game? Explain why or why not.

Name ____

Postcards from Two Places

If you went back in time and visited Santo Domingo, and then Maine, at the time of "Cocoa Ice," you would want to send everyone postcards to tell about your amazing trips!

trading schooner harvest machete pulp bargain support

What you need:

- index cards
- pencil
- crayons or markers

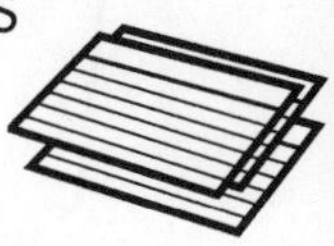

What to do:

1. Write a postcard to a friend that tells what you did and saw in Santo Domingo. Use the Vocabulary Words to help you describe things you saw and did. Decorate the other side of the card with a picture of life in Santa Domingo, based on what you read in the story.

2. Now make a postcard about your trip to Maine. Make sure that you use each Vocabulary Word on at least one of the postcards.

Name ______________________________

Which Would You Rather Do?

This story describes two different ways to do things in two different parts of the world. Which do you like better?

What you need:

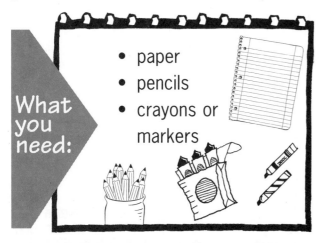

- paper
- pencils
- crayons or markers

What to do:

1. Fold a piece of paper in half. Write *Cocoa Ice* at the top of one half. Then write *Chocolate Ice Cream* at the top of the other half.

2. Find the part of the story that tells how to make cocoa ice. Write down each step in the cocoa ice half of your paper. Include the things you need to make it. Based on what's said in the story, tell what the cocoa ice is like. Do the same thing for chocolate ice cream.

3. Choose a color to circle the things that are alike in each of the two processes. Use another color to circle the things that are different in each process. Write a key at the bottom of the page that tells what each color means.

4. Write a brief paragraph that sums up what is alike and what is different about the processes. Tell which you would rather do. Think about the end result when you choose the one you would like to do!

Name ______________________________

Pass It On

When you hear something and then retell it in your own words, you are *paraphrasing*. How do things change when several people retell each other's words?

What you need:

- index cards
- pencil

What to do:

1. Find the part of the story that tells how the family in Santo Domingo harvests and prepares cocoa beans. Read it over carefully. Using your own words, write the cocoa bean process on an index card.

2. Read your version of the cocoa bean process. Using that version, retell it in your own words again. Make sure you use the version on your card, not the one in the story.

3. Compare both your versions to the original in the story. What stayed the same? What changed? Did you still get all the important information? Did you always use your own words? Write a paragraph that explains what you learned.

Name ______________________________

Word Machines

Words help us identify things and express ideas, thoughts, and feelings. What if there were machines that took the place of words?

choices	**congratulations**	**value**
amount	**receive**	**combinations**

What you need:

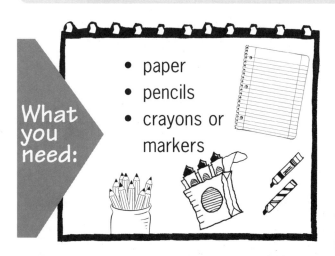

- paper
- pencils
- crayons or markers

What to do:

1. Invent a machine that does what each Vocabulary Word means. For example, a "Congratulations Robot" would go around shaking people's hands and telling them, "Good work!" A "Choices Switch" could show different choices in a situation every time it is turned on.

2. Draw a picture of each of your word machines. Underneath, write a description of what it does. Make sure your description and machine show the meaning of the word.

3. Put your pictures together into a booklet. Draw a cover, and give it a title such as "Words That Work."

Name ______________________________

It's in the Details

The main idea is the most important part of a paragraph or passage. Sometimes the main idea is not stated, but you can find it in the details.

What you need:

- paper
- pencil

What to do:

1. Imagine that you have been asked to do a household chore that you dislike, such as cleaning the kitchen or raking the leaves. You might even choose an imaginary chore like washing the spaceboat or sweeping stardust!

2. Write a letter to a friend explaining that you cannot play because you have to do the chore. In the letter, use details about the chore to try to get your friend to help you finish the chore, *without* asking for his or her help. You might talk about how much faster the chore would be completed by two people or why two people could do the job better than one.

3. On a separate piece of paper, answer the following questions about your letter:

- What is the stated main idea of the letter?
- What is the *unstated* main idea of the letter?
- What details in the letter help you find the unstated main idea?

Name ______________________________

Picture This

Sometimes you may take spelling tests where you have to choose correctly or incorrectly spelled words in a group. For this kind of test, it helps if you have a picture in your mind of how certain kinds of words should look.

What you need:

- crayons or markers
- paper
- pencil

What to do:

1. Look for words in "If You Made a Million" that have easily confused prefixes or suffixes, such as *im–* and *in–* or *–ible* and *–able.*

2. Divide these words into teams based on their common beginnings or endings. For example, you might choose words that begin with *im–* or words that end with *–able.* Write each team on its own sheet of paper, and give each team its own color. Think of a name for the team that will help you remember the correct beginning or ending for that whole group, such as the "Impossibles" or the "Remarkables."

3. Study each list independently. Make sure you understand the meaning of each word on the team. Remember each team's color and name.

Name ______________________________

t's a Match!

Test your memory and understanding of the Vocabulary Words by playing the Vocabulary Match Game.

signal **celebrations** **choosy** **average** **tracks** **admiring**

What you need:

- pencil
- index cards

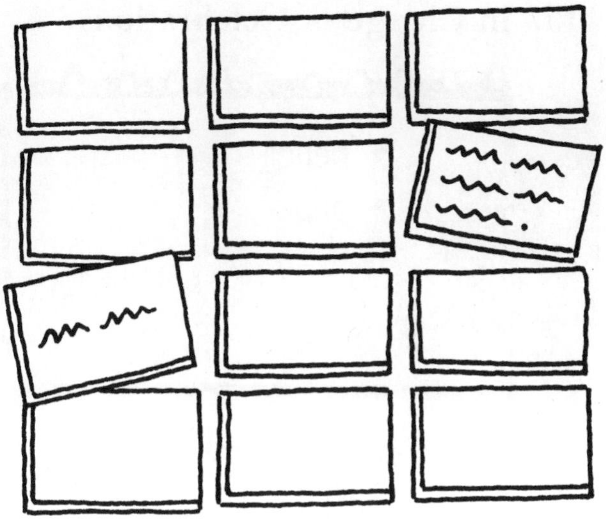

What to do:

1. Write each Vocabulary Word on the front of an index card. Then write the definitions of the words on six different cards.

2. Shuffle all the cards. Place the cards face down on the floor or table. Place them in three columns of four cards each.

3. Flip over two cards at a time. If you turn over a word and its definition, take the cards, and use the word in a sentence. If not, turn both cards back over. Try to remember where the cards are so that you have a better chance to match the word with its definition next time.

Name ______________________________

Newsflash: Girl Creates Her Own Holidays!

Reporters often use summaries to create news stories. Newspaper reporters must write the main points of a story in a certain amount of space. Television reporters have to tell their stories in a short amount of time. When you summarize, you briefly tell what something is about. Imagine that you are a television reporter doing a story on the girl from "I'm in Charge of Celebrations."

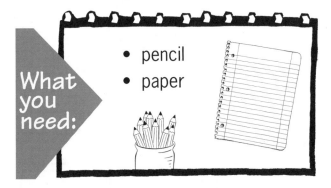

What you need:

- pencil
- paper

What to do:

1. Write the questions *Who? What? Where?* and *When?* along the left side of a piece of paper.

2. Answer each question with a few words or sentences. Explain who the girl is, where she lives, and what she does. For *When?*, write down the dates of a few of the holidays, and explain them briefly.

3. Write a short news article about the girl, using your notes to help you.

Name ______________________________

Desert Dictionary

Alejandro lives in the desert. Make a Desert Dictionary to help other readers understand what happens in "Alejandro's Gift."

windmill   cherished   furrows   ample   shunned   growth

What you need:

- crayons or markers
- paper

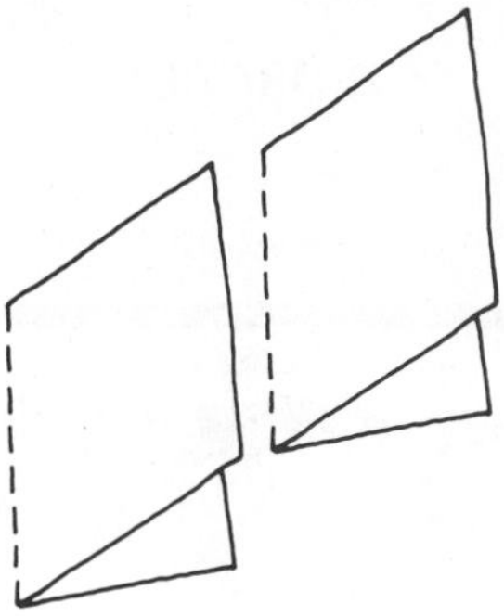

What to do:

1. Fold a few pieces of paper in half to make a book. Draw a cover for your Desert Dictionary on the front.

2. Write the Vocabulary Words in alphabetical order inside the book.

3. Write the definitions of the Vocabulary Words. You can draw pictures to go with your definitions. Then write a sentence using each Vocabulary Word.

Name ______________________________

Then What Happened?

Stories are long chains of causes and effects. By writing a sequence of cause-and-effect statements, you can write a crazy story of your own!

What you need:

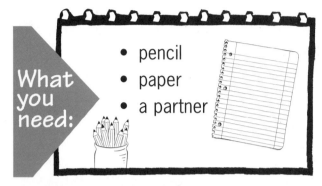

- pencil
- paper
- a partner

What to do:

1. On the first line of your paper, write *C*. This stands for *cause*. Write a statement that could be a cause. Exchange papers with a partner. Write *E* on the next line, after your partner's cause, for *effect*. Then write a sentence that could be an effect of the cause. Exchange papers again.

2. Read what your partner wrote on your paper. Then continue the story, adding another cause statement. Keep exchanging papers. See how funny you can make the stories!

C The monkey saw a banana.

E He ran for the banana.

C The monkey didn't see the banana peel on the ground.

E He slipped on the peel.

C He grabbed for something to keep himself from falling.

E He accidentally pulled the lever on the ice cream machine.

C Ice cream started flying around the room.

Name ______________________________

What's My Word?

Have you ever played Charades? Charades is a game where you act out words while other players guess them. In this game, you will draw pictures instead.

magma edges range epicenter coast peak

What you need:

- index cards
- paper
- markers or crayons

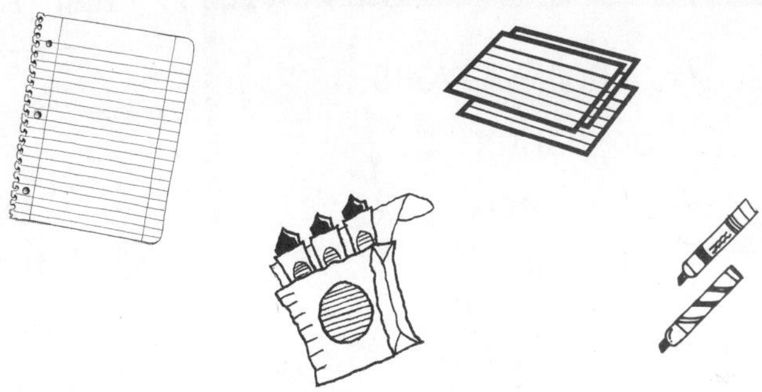

What to do:

1. Write each Vocabulary Word on an index card. Below the word, draw a picture that helps show the meaning. Write the definition on the back.

2. Use the cards to test yourself, and shuffle them after each round. You can also test yourself by starting with the definition.

3. Write each Vocabulary Word in a sentence.

Name ______________________________

You're the Author

Imagine that you are an author writing a book on one of your favorite subjects. You'll need a title page, a few sentences about your topic, an index, and a glossary.

What you need:

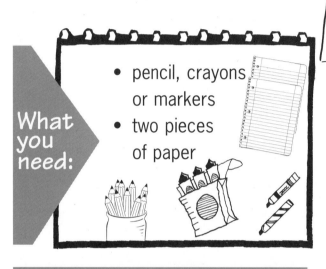

- pencil, crayons or markers
- two pieces of paper

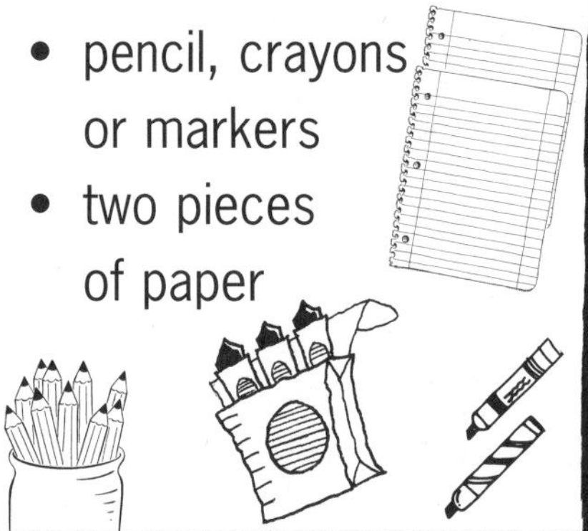

What to do:

1. Fold the pieces of paper in half to make a book. Write the title of your book and your name on the front page. Open the book when you are done.

2. Write your story on the first two inside pages. Write a few paragraphs. Include drawings, if you like. Label the left side *1* and the right side *2*. Turn the page when you are done.

Index

Beds *2*	Pets *1*
Cats *1, 2*	Sofas *2*
Fish *1*	Sun *2*

3. Write *Index* at the top of the left page. Then, go back and find some nouns in your story. List them in alphabetical order, and write whether they are on page 1, 2, or 1 and 2.

4. Write *Glossary* on the top of the right page. Define a few of the words that you used that might be challenging for other readers.

Glossary

Beds—places to sleep
Cats—furry animals with pointy ear
Fish—animals that swim and live in the water
Sofa—a couch